Swim or Drown

Business and Life Lessons I've Learned from the Ocean

Warren Cassell Jr.

Published by FastPencil

To My Wonderful Parents, Cleo & Warren.
Thank you for allowing me to chase my dreams.

৯৬

Contents

Acknowledgements

With the deepest gratitude I wish to thank Samuel Engelen, who professionally edited and helped to make *Swim or Drown* suitable for publication.

I would also like to acknowledge and express my gratitude to the following people for their valuable feedback: Allen Mullings, Curtis Knee, Josh Lipovetsky, Madeleine Richey, Mohammed Islam, Robert Longley, Tahlia Meredith and Zachariah Westerfield.

If you spot any typos or grammatical mistakes, it is probably due to me ignoring their great advice.

CHAPTER 1

Thought-Provoking Realization

> 66 Study nature, love nature, stay close to nature. It will never fail you."

– Frank Lloyd Wright

At the age of thirteen, I came to a fascinating conclusion about life. As a result, my entire perception of the world and how I thought it worked had completely changed. I was convinced that, when shared, my thought-provoking realization would resolve most, if not all, of today's most painful and redundant problems.

As I thought more and more about what I had learned, I began researching and found that I was not the only one who had reached this conclusion. Aristotle, The Buddha, Lao Tzu, Heraclitus, Confucius, Ralph Waldo Emerson, Rembrandt, Alan Watts, Walt Whitman, George Washington Carver, Oprah Winfrey and Max Ehrmann all knew the same thing I had discovered. All of them even shared it through their teachings, essays, poems and other works.

What did I discover? It occurred to me that nature is constantly trying to teach us something. Whether it is about the way we handle our circumstances, the way we deal with others or the way we go about our day-to-day lives. The birds, the plants and even the rain all have a message for us. Nature is a source of unlimited knowledge!

I became compulsive about documenting everything that I saw because I was confident that my surroundings were always carrying a message for me to discover. I watched countless documentaries on animals. I became highly knowledgeable about plants and the many different functions and features of nature. I observed the movements of every creature that was in my presence. And as I analyzed my observations I couldn't believe what I had found. The content that can be found in personal growth books, the lessons that are taught at self-help seminars and even investing and success principles are all aligned with what I observed in nature and the lives of other animals. When we adopt the lifestyle of nature we position ourselves closer to achieving success—wealth, health and happiness!

In 2013, I shared my thoughts on nature with the world, with the launch of my blog, ZapSocial.co [http://www.zap-social.co/], and through the release of my first book, *The Farm of Wisdom*.

With this book, I hope to push my message even further by taking you on a diving trip to explore life under our oceans. I came across a fun fact that said only five percent of our waters have been explored and then a light bulb went off …

Who knows how much we can learn from the undiscovered depths of the ocean!

After reading Swim or Drown, you will be more knowledgeable about what actually goes on in our waters and you'll be able to cultivate these lessons in your personal and business life.

I hope that my effort will change your perception of nature, and especially of the ocean, because sharks, turtles, squids, and even plankton can teach us how to succeed in life and business.

Best,

Warren Cassell, Jr.

CHAPTER 2

Time to Discover

The morning has just begun and thousands of newly hatched sea turtles are eagerly digging their way to the surface of the sand to tell the Earth hello. However, it's only a few moments after greeting the world that these creatures realize that their first day on the planet will also be their longest and most precarious.

Before they can reach the safety of the sea, these hatchlings need to escape the dangers of the predators that surround the nesting area. Only five out of one hundred turtles will reach the ocean and the other ninety-five will soon become lunch for birds, raccoons and even crabs.

Despite this grim prospect, these creatures are ready to take up the challenge. Several sea turtles sprint across the beach, jumping over driftwood and dodging hungry birds. These creatures simply do not know the meaning of the word "obstacle."

Focused on their goal, they don't look back; they ignore whatever hurdles that are in their path. They move confidently through the sand, defying the predators, and are determined to reach the ocean.

~

This is just one of the infinite lessons that we can learn from the ocean and use in our business and personal life to attain happiness, wealth, and health. Just think about it: if baby sea turtles can encourage us to conquer obstacles, what can bigger and more developed sea creatures teach us?

Nearly three-quarters of the earth's surface is covered by the ocean and more than ninety-five percent of life on earth is aquatic—yet humans have only explored about five percent of the ocean. Imagine the amount of undiscovered wisdom that hides under the deep blue sea.

If you read this book carefully you will be able to understand that nature offers us a wealth of knowledge and that the ocean holds an abundance of success principles. In addition, you will learn about the many species that inhabit our oceans.

If you adopt and cultivate the habits and principles from the aquatic animals exposed in this book, you will be better able to position yourself to achieve a life of abundance, happiness and health.

The aim of this book is not to dictate to you a set of habits that must be followed in order to attain success in business and life. Instead, it aims to outline a few of the endless principles that can be learned from the sea and its inhabitants. Rather than making *Swim or Drown* your doctrine, make it a reminder that when we observe the life of our fellow earthlings we can learn a lot.

During the writing process of *Swim or Drown* it was very important to get rid of the usual fluff often found in books. This book presents information in a very concise and short way, ensuring that each sentence is meaningful, memorable and shareable.

For those who are ready to attain wealth, to succeed in their business career and to lead a happy and meaningful life, I offer you a challenge: From now on, turn to nature for answers, observe the life of other earthlings and be willing to adopt the principles that animals and plants live by.

CHAPTER 3

Swim or Drown

> ❝ He who is silent is forgotten; he who abstains is taken at his word; he who does not advance, falls back; he who stops is overwhelmed, distanced, crushed; he who ceases to grow greater becomes smaller; he who leaves off, gives up; the stationary condition is the beginning of the end—it is the terrible symptom which precedes death."

- Henri-Frédéric Amielx

When we think about the lessons that the ocean and its inhabitants can teach us about success, sharks are almost always one of the first creatures that cross our minds. They are one of the fiercest animals on the planet and have no natural predators.

Most people will think of the shark as an utterly dominating force of nature, almost invincible. In the business world, a 'shark' is someone who goes after what he wants with a total disregard for others and seemingly without a conscience.

However, this is partly due to the unfair picture the media has shown us about sharks. Yes, they're carnivorous and they are highly efficient predators. But they're not nearly as dangerous and threatening as some would have us believe.

In fact, statistically, there's a higher chance of being killed by a vending machine than a shark. You're also much more likely to get struck by lightning. Of course, it all depends on where you spend your days (around vending machines or in the open ocean?), but the point is that sharks have gotten an undeserved ill reputation.

Here's a lesser-known fact about sharks that might help shift your perspective: Sharks move water across their gills by swimming. Water flows in through their mouths, across their gills, and out through their gill slits. In order to survive, sharks must continuously swim to breathe. Stopping would cause them to die.

Sharks don't wait for their next meal to come to them and neither should you. Likewise, when your first catch isn't successful you shouldn't give up. Usually, when the thought of quitting comes to mind we are only a few steps away from success.

But what does it mean to keep moving forward? Moving forward simply means looking at our past decisions, evaluating our mistakes and using our observations to swim into the best suitable waters. However, don't mistake the words 'keep moving forward' for 'don't pause.' Pausing gives us time to think and prepare for new waters. In fact, pausing is just another form of moving forward. Not taking time to slow down and listen to what our past mistakes, our present circumstances and nature as a whole are telling us is just as bad as moving forward without giving ourselves time to rest for new ideas to be conceived in our minds.

Even if you feel comfortable and content doing what you are doing every day without any change, it is still vital that you try something new. It does not matter if your company has been able to bring in steady profits without the need for changes. Your company will never be able to maximize the talent of its staff if you never take the risk to invest in new ventures; therefore, you will not be able to take income to the next level. Not taking the opportunity and losing the lesson is far worse than failing once and losing some money.

Similarly, if you have been working in a company for ten years and you are doing your job exactly the same way you did when you started you are just wasting space! How will you ever discover new things about yourself if you do not swim further with new ways to work? Your boss will never think differently about you if you don't experiment with your style of work. Not moving forward in your job makes it easy for your opinions and ideas to drown in the waves of those people in the company who are brave enough to swim in new waters.

If you don't move forward with your girlfriend of so many years and don't propose, sooner rather than later she will swim away to someone else. And if you express your love to your partner the conventional way, your relationship will grow stale and your feelings for each other will fizzle out. Those who don't move forward get lost in the current.

Much more than a simple analogy, 'swim or drown' is a reminder that when we don't move forward with our relationships, continuously explore new waters of our personal lives and add new ideas drop by drop to our businesses, we only kill them slowly. Never stop moving forward and don't be afraid to discover new waters. Swim or drown—you decide.

CHAPTER 4

Come Up For Air

> 66 Even with a busy schedule of eating, swimming, and napping, sea turtles always make time to pop up above the surface to take a breath. If you tend to get bogged down in the details of a problem or a project, do yourself a favor and come up for air."

- Winona Dimeo-Ediger

Although whales, manatees, dolphins, seals, orcas and sea otters spend most of their time either in or around the ocean, they are not fish, despite what most people think. They are actually mammals, just like you and me. These creatures have a lot of the same characteristics as humans, including being warm-blooded, having mammary glands that produce milk, and they even nurture their young.

Here's a crazy fact I learned in Biology class recently: Despite the fact that whales and seals live in the ocean, they are more related to us humans than, say, crocodiles or even chickens. Pretty cool, huh?

Sea mammals spend most of their days underwater, but because they have lungs they regularly have to come up to the surface to take a new breath of fresh air. If they don't, they will drown beneath the waves of the sea. Sea mammals and turtles (turtles are reptiles and not mammals, but still would drown if they did not pop up to the surface for air) can remind us that when life seems to be drowning us, we should come up to the surface for a new breath, a new perspective and a refreshed body.

In these busy times, it's not unusual for a day's work to include responding to countless emails, making hundreds of phone calls and attending half a dozen meetings, while studying for a part-time course, juggling a complicated relationship or trying to support a friend, and barely managing to squeeze in a few hours of good night's rest. Let's face it: Life cannot be enjoyed if all we do is keep ourselves busy. Just like sea mammals, we will drown if we don't come up for air.

Most occupations require people to constantly keep working (or at least pretend to be working). This is why it is extremely important to work in a career that you are passionate about, because if you don't, you will feel unmotivated. However, even if you love what you do for a living, coming up for air is extremely important as it allows you to rest, review your past decisions and potentially spot flaws that would not have been seen in a stressful environment.

As mentioned in an earlier chapter, taking a moment to slow down is a form of moving forward, and moving forward is a key factor to achieving success. Think of a hedge fund manager who took a four-week vacation in Barbados, not to forget about the bad trades he made for the year, but to come out of the intense environment of the trading ground to analyze his mistakes and make better decisions. He would not have been able to get a clear view of what went wrong in the screaming and heated environment of the stock exchange trading floor. He was able to move forward while taking it slow.

Come up for air. It's a very simple statement but also a very easy one to forget. If you're afraid that taking it slow will disconnect you from your work, it could mean that you aren't passionate enough about your job. If you are truly passionate, disconnection will not happen. Do not be afraid to surface every now and then. It helps lessen the distractions of your regular life, leaving a lot of space in your mind for new thoughts to flow in and out.

CHAPTER 5

Evolve and Adapt for Efficiency

66 We all grow and we all change, it's the natural cycle of
life. We will always be continually evolving within ourselves."

- Bianca Strom

In the previous chapter, you learned that whales and dolphins were mammals. This means that, like us, they
breathe air into their lungs, are warm-blooded, feed their
young milk and some of them even have hair (although
very little). But don't let their streamlined bodies or their
flippers fool you; both whales and dolphins were once land
animals with legs! They began to look for food in the
ocean and over a (very, very long) period of time adapted
to aquatic conditions.

Actually, a lot has changed in the ocean since it was first
formed more than three and a half billion years ago. The

conditions of the Earth were also very different than the ones we now enjoy. As time passed and the conditions on Earth slowly changed, life under the sea—from the tiniest microscopic bacteria to more complex creatures and even aquatic plants—had to adapt to these changes in order to live comfortably in these new environments.

The same can be said for our lives. Every second of the day, something changes within and around us, and we can only thrive and survive if we adapt to these constant changes that are occurring in our businesses, friendships, love life, etc. And even if you think these changes are insignificant or you don't even notice them, just look at yourself now and compare that with who you were ten or even five years ago. You are surely not the same person you were in the past and this is because these constant self-changes have transformed you into the person you are today.

What causes these changes? When we read new things, it is possible that we change our beliefs on how the world works. For example, after reading this book you will probably be more conscious of nature and your fellow earthlings.

Sometimes, change is brought about by bad experiences. We might offer help to someone who shows no appreciation in the end. After that experience we might try to prevent history from repeating itself by closing up and not being as caring as we used to be.

In business, change can be caused by a shift in the demand of what consumers want. Adapting to changes in the market is vital to the life of the business. Being ignorant of the fact that the world around us is not stable and resisting the natural change in business causes many organizations to fail.

Our constant evolution causes us to lose things and people that were once close to our heart. The most common result of change in relationships is that the frequencies that were once connected between partners lose synchronization. As one partner learns new things and shifts his/her sails, it sometimes causes the other partner to "fall out of love."

Companies can lose customers when they adapt to change. An increase in pricing for services may cause customers to run to the competition. Dropping a product may also result in customers leaving.

Yes, change sometimes causes loss and yes, it can hurt. But we should not resist change. Whether we like it or not, we will evolve, and resisting evolution will just make the process harder. Hey, the whale had to give up its legs to live in the cool ocean!

In the ocean, as the environment transforms (whether due to a change in temperature or a loss of a food source) the animals in that environment naturally adapt to these changes. The world around us isn't stable and if we resist adaptation, we risk not being able to cope with the ever-changing world. Evolution is a sign of life and progress; it makes us wiser people and it shouldn't be resisted. What I came to realize is that the more in tune we are with nature and the more we actually observe our surroundings, the easier it is for us to adapt to change which results in more effective evolution.

CHAPTER 6

Focus On Your Unique Strengths

66   There are countless worlds and there are countless
best."

- Mike Michalowicz

When we look at the ocean, it's sometimes hard to remember that beneath the beautiful blue surface, there are countless creatures. Each with its own unique strengths and talents. There are fish that can swim as fast as cars, and there are fish that are able to survive in extremely cold or hot waters. Some sea creatures are naturally good at hunting prey, while others have mastered the art of tricking their predators with camouflage. These countless survival abilities that aquatic animals possess make it impossible to name one particular creature the dominant one. Because each creature has its own area of strength and lives in different environments and conditions, it may not need the features and abilities that others may need.

This is a mistake that a lot of us make in our lives: We don't recognize that there are countless categories to be the best at, and endless worlds for us to choose from to dominate. Being at the top of an area really depends on how broad or narrow you define that area to be.

It's hard to say what the dominant sea creature is, but crowning each creature for their field of strength is easy! The cuttlefish and seahorse may be called the masters of underwater camouflage and mantis shrimp have excellent vision (much better color vision than humans—their eyes have twelve types of color receptors, while humans have only three!).

It's just like trying to generalize who the top child in the class is. It wouldn't necessarily be the most well-behaved student or the kid with the best grades. It would be more appropriate to narrow it down into specific categories like mathematical intelligence, creativity, determination, etc.

An example in business would be the clothing industry. If we define this area as general clothing (not narrowing it down into different niches) and use profits as the measuring stick, it's probably chain stores that are at the top. However, if we use brand recognition or prestige as the scale for the best, high-end fashion companies will come out on top. And if we measure by quality, much smaller companies might rise to the top.

What I realized was, if there are countless areas for one to be the best at, there is no need for you to outsmart your co-workers for your boss to notice you. Instead, you can do what you do best and you'll be recognized as the leader in your area of strength.

Likewise, you don't necessarily need to crush every competitor to be on top. When you recognize that there are infinite worlds that you can dominate, you won't need to pour boiling oil on the competition to succeed; if you offer something unique and different, you are already on top of that category.

The "top player" is merely an illusion and impossible to determine, because we all offer our unique features and strengths. It's hard to say what factors determine a person or company to be the best. Think of it this way: Even if you don't believe that humans are the "dominant" species, I'm sure you don't think that cockroaches are stronger than us…. But scientists have proven that they can actually survive a nuclear bomb attack! Despite this fact, I'm sure I would be called crazy if I said that cockroaches were one of the planet's top organisms.

By developing our own unique strengths and talents, we keep the ecology of the human world diverse and healthy, and there's no need for anyone to claim a generalized top position. This way, we have to work together to make the system function.

CHAPTER 7

Embrace Symbiotic Relationships

Symbiosis (n)

interaction between two different organisms living in close physical association.

I recently came across symbiosis, which is the name given to a relationship between two different species that live together. An example would be flowers and bees: Flowers provide food for bees, while bees help to pollinate flowers. Without bees, many flowers would not be able to produce seeds. That's an example of symbiosis on land; but make no mistake, a lot of aquatic creatures depend on symbiotic relationships for survival.

The two most widely recognized types of symbiosis are parasitism and mutualism. When I learned this, I instantly made a connection to our lives. Parasitism is the name given to non-mutual relationships where one organism (the parasite) benefits at the expense of the host. There are a lot of parasitic relationships under the ocean. An example of such a relationship would be sea lampreys and fish. Sea lampreys are slimy, snake-like creatures that have a suction cup mouth filled with sharp teeth. They attach to fish and feed on their blood. Fish that are attacked by sea lampreys aren't able to free themselves from these deadly creatures and usually end up dead because of the loss of blood and nutrients. The fish that do survive attacks are left with a large wounds that can easily become infected.

Although present under the ocean, parasitism can be found in the lives of humans as well. Parasitism between humans tends to be more emotional and mental, rather than physical (unless you believe in vampires, or, you know, we have a zombie apocalypse). Being surrounded by people who let off large amounts of negative energy can be considered a parasitic environment. Unfortunately, a lot of romantic relationships are parasitic, leaving one partner fully nourished by sucking all of the other partner's energy. If you notice that your friendship, your intimate relationship with your partner or even the professional relationship with one of your clients is parasitic, you need to find a way out. Parasitic relationships will only cause you harm.

Mutualism, a relationship between two species in which both benefit from the association, can also be found under the ocean as well as in our lives, both personal and business. These are the relationships that we should try to make and keep, because they allow us to give and receive value.

If you've seen Finding Nemo (and really, who hasn't?) you've witnessed one of the most beautiful examples of mutualism in the ocean. Nemo and his father were both clownfish living within anemones. Sea anemones have tentacles that sting. Clownfish have a layer of mucus on their skin which protects them from the stinging tentacles of sea anemones. Predators of the clownfish are unable to withstand the sting of the tentacles. As a result, clownfish are able to hide and rest within the anemones safely. In return, the clownfish scares off other fish, like the butterfly fish, which eat sea anemones when clownfish aren't present. There is also evidence to suggest that waste materials from clownfish serve as a source of nutrients to anemones. In this relationship, both organisms benefit.

Likewise, our personal lives and businesses are dependent on relationships with others. Greatness can not be achieved without the input of others. It's the truth; I dare you to name any person or company that contributed to society without the help of others. Completely self-made men are nothing but myths.

There are a number of symbiotic relationships that happen under the ocean. Actually, all organisms are interdependent on other species. Without interaction between different organisms the whole ecological system would die and this is a wonderful reminder to us humans that we should recognize the importance of relationships, because all of us—land animals, sea creatures, humans, and even companies—are built on symbiotic relationships, and since we are first and foremost social creatures, this is especially important to us. When we recognize how vital it is to create and nurture relationships and when we begin to swim away from parasitic friends and embrace mutualistic relationships, we create an opportunity to reach greatness.

CHAPTER 8

Use What You've Got

66 Start where you are. Use what you have. Do what you can."

- Arthur Ashe

"You don't have to be great to start, but you have to start to be great."

- Zig Ziglar

Have you ever heard of a type of fish called the cavefish? They are small in size, pink in color, live in caves at the bottom of the ocean, and oh yeah, they have no sense of sight! Their ancestors were normal fish with eyes, but somewhere along the evolution of the cavefish, their visual organs disappeared. Despite this, these fish are excellent navigators. In fact, when they travel in groups, they don't even bump into each other. After reading about the cavefish, I researched even more about them and found that there were countless fish that are able to feed and reproduce just fine without vision. It is possible for them to hunt and survive because they use what they have—their sense of taste, touch and smell—to their advantage.

And this is just one example. No one organism has everything. Seahorses are horrible swimmers. Added to that they don't have any defense mechanism, yet they aren't miserable about it. Instead of focusing on what they don't have, they use their remarkable camouflaging technique to their advantage. Don't think that their swimming disability is bad for the seahorse; instead, think about it this way: While fish who are better at swimming swim away from their predators, the seahorse is able to hide from their predator in plain sight.

There's a saying that goes, "No one has everything but everyone has something." My interpretation of this saying is this: Everyone has something to start with, and because everyone has something we ought to be grateful for what we have, no matter how little we think it is. The truth is, nothing is too small to lead us to greatness. And I believe that the best way to show appreciation for what you have is to make the most of it. Seahorses aren't able to outswim predators, but they use what they have to stay alive.

A lot of us don't realize that the ocean, which covers ninety-five percent of our planet, is made up of tiny drops of water. It all started with something small. Every day several people get million-dollar ideas, yet very few align those ideas with action. They wait for the perfect moment, for everything to be "in place." Sadly, the perfect moment is an illusion, and no one will ever be able to start with everything they want. As a result those people with million-dollar ideas wait forever.

When we start with passion and with a clear understanding of what we have and where we need to go, what we lack is not important. We can achieve whatever we want, but only if we start to move toward that goal. Waiting for what doesn't exist will not help us get what we want. What will bring us closer is our appreciation of what we already have.

If you have an idea for the next bestseller, start to write! Don't wait for a better plot to come along or for your network to expand or for an agent's approval. Write, start with that story idea that you have, and do the same if you have a multi-million dollar idea. Why would you possibly want to stall it?

It's amazing how these little creatures, the cavefish and the seahorse, can teach us such a powerful lesson. It is important to forget what you lack and find a way for you to use what you have. What I've come to realize is, as long as you are passionate about what you do, the things you'll need will show up eventually. When the things you want don't show up, it simply means that you don't need them. Go out there and be the best you can be, with the things you have.

CHAPTER 9

Discover New Oceans

> *Man cannot discover new oceans unless he has the courage to lose sight of the shore.*"

– Andre Gide

When I set out to write this book, I had one goal in mind: I wanted more people to understand that nature holds a lot of lessons for us. This is something I discovered at a very early age, and ever since I became more observant of my surroundings, a lot of things have become clear to me. I learned new ways to deal with problems and I took a new approach to life in general. I chose to explore the ocean with my readers in *Swim or Drown* because I couldn't find what better ecosystem to learn lessons from. Humans have only explored five percent of the ocean!

Hopefully, you've enjoyed our diving trip. This book was intentionally short. I wanted to share a handful of the lessons I learned from life under the sea. My aim was to get you to start thinking about nature and its lessons. Instead of writing a long book with a multitude of lessons, I wanted to inspire you to be more observant so that you could unlock these secrets yourself.

Overall, nature has principles that work together to form successful organisms. If we took these same principles and implemented them in our own lives, we would become highly efficient individuals.

Your task now is to go outside and unlock new lessons and discover new oceans.

About the Author

Warren Cassell, Jr. is the author of *The Farm of Wisdom* and *Swim or Drown*. At the age of eight, with a capital investment from his mom and dad, he launched his own greeting card and graphic design company.

After this, Warren embarked on a number of other ventures including an application development firm and a web hosting service provider. By the time he was thirteen years old, he had been investing in companies and doing business with firms and clients all over the world.

With a business and investment portfolio ranging from financial services and media to Internet and food manufacturing, it is safe to say that Warren is the living proof of the fact that anyone with a vision, determination and dedication can achieve great success.

www.ingramcontent.com/pod-product-compliance
Lightning Source LLC
Chambersburg PA
CBHW071327310526
45789CB00016B/1698